Alexander
BORODIN

POLOVSTIAN DANCES
(Prince Igor, Act II)
Edited by
Richard W. Sargeant, Jr.

Study Score
Partitur

SERENISSIMA MUSIC, INC.

ORCHESTRA

Piccolo

2 Flutes

2 Oboes (2nd also English Horn)

2 Clarinets (B-flat and A)

2 Bassoons

4 Horns (F)

2 Trumpets (C)*

3 Trombones

Tuba

Timpani

Percussion

Snare Drum, Triangle, Tanbourine,

Cymbals, Bass Drum, Glockenspiel

Harp

Violin I

Violin II

Viola

Violoncello

Double Bass

*The present score has been updated for the commonkeys of modern instruments
(Clarinets in A or B-flat, Horns in F, Trumpets in C). The original score featured
Trumpets in B-flat and A.

Duration: ca. 15 minutes

Premiere: November 4, 1890 (in Act II of *Prince Igor*)
St. Petersburg
Maryinsky Theatre
Chorus, Orchestra / Karl Kuchera

ISMN: 979-0-58042-110-4
This score is anewly-engraved edition based upon the the first edition
full score and parts issued 1888 by M.P. Belaieff, Leipzig.

Printed in the USA
First Printing: August, 2018

POLOVTSIAN DANCES
from 'Prince Igor'
1.

Alexander Borodin
Orchestration by Nikolay Rimsky-Korsakov
Edited by Richard W. Sargeant, Jr.

42226

11
Picc.
Fl. 1 2
p
Ob. 1 2
Cl. 1
Cl. 2
Bn. 1 2
Hn. 1 2
Hn. 3 4
Timp.
Tamb.
Tgl.
Cymb.
11
Vn. 1
Vn. 2
div.
Va.
Vc.
Cb.

21
29
Picc.
mf
Fl. 1 2
1.
mf
Ob. 1 2
mf
Cl.
1
2
p
p
f
Bn. 1 2
1.
mf
Hn.
1 2
3 4
mf
Timp.
p
Tamb.
Tgl.
Cymb.
29
21
(pizz.)
Vn.
1
mf
2
unis.
Va.
mf
Vc.
mf
Cb.

31
Picc.
Fl. 1 2
Ob. 1 2
Cl. 1 2
mf
mf
Bn. 1 2
Hn. 1 2 3 4
Timp.
Tamb.
Tgl. Cymb.
31
div.
Vn. 1 2
Va.
Vc.
Cb.

41
Picc.
Fl. 1 2
Ob. 1 2
Cl. 1 2
Bn. 1 2
Hn. 1 2 3 4
Timp.
Tamb.
Tgl. Cymb.
Vn. 1 2
Va.
Vc.
Cb.
cresc.
f
ff
sfp
sf
pizz.

50
53
Picc.
Fl. 1 2
a2
mf
Ob. 1 2
f
Cl. 1
Cl. 2
p
Bn. 1 2
Hn. 1 2
Hn. 3 4
Timp.
mf
Tamb.
Tgl. Cymb.
pp
50
53
Vn. 1
arco unis.
sf
pp
Vn. 2
div.
sf
pp
Va.
sf
sf
arco
p
Vc.
sf
Cb.
(pizz.)
sf

59
Picc.
Fl. 1 2
Ob. 1 2
Cl. 1 2
Bn. 1 2
Hn. 1 2 3 4
Timp.
Tamb.
Tgl. Cymb.
59
Vn. 1 2
Va.
Vc.
arco
p
Cb.

71
67
Picc.
Fl. 1 2
Ob. 1 2
mf
Cl. 1 2
Bn. 1 2
p
Hn. 1 2 3 4
1.
p
Timp.
Tamb.
Tgl. Cymb.
2
4
71
67
Vn. 1 2
p
arco unis.
p
Va.
Vc.
Cb.

75
Picc.
Fl. 1 2
Ob. 1 2
Cl. (B♭) 1 2
Bn. 1 2
Hn. 1 2
3 4
Timp.
Tamb.
Tgl. Cymb.
Vn. 1
2
Va.
Vc.
Cb.
mf
a2
mf marc.
pp

91
84
Picc.
cresc. poco a poco
Fl. 1 2
Ob. 1 2
Cl. (B♭) 1 2
Bn. 1 2
f marc.
Hn. 1 2 3 4
Timp.
Tamb.
poco f
Tgl. Cymb.
Vn. 1 2
spicato assai
Va.
Vc.
Cb.
arco

93
Picc.
Fl. 1 2
Ob. 1 2
Cl. (B♭) 1 2
Bn. 1 2
a2
Hn. 1 2 3 4
Timp.
Tamb.
Tgl. Cymb.
poco f
Vn. 1 2
Va.
Vc.
Cb.

103
Picc.
Fl. 1 2
Ob. 1 2
Cl. (B♭) 1 2
Bn. 1 2
Hn. 1 2
3 4
Timp.
Tamb.
Tgl. Cymb.
Vn. 1
2
Va.
Vc.
Cb.
mp con forza
p
poco f
pizz.
p dolce

113
Picc.
Fl. 1 2
Ob. 1 2
p cresc.
Cl. (B♭) 1 2
cresc.
Bn. 1 2
cresc.
1.
p cresc.
Hn. 1 2 3 4
Timp.
Tamb.
Tgl. Cymb.
p cresc. poco
113
arco
Vn. 1
cresc.
arco
2
cresc.
arco
Va.
cresc.
Vc.
cresc.
Cb.

122
129
Picc.
mf
Fl. 1 2
a2
f
sf
Ob. 1 2
Cl. (B♭) 1 2
p
Bn. 1 2
Hn. 1 2
Hn. 3 4
Timp.
sfp
Tamb.
Tgl. Cymb.
Vn. 1
Vn. 2
Va.
pizz.
mf
Vc.
Cb.

131
Picc.
Fl. 1 2
p
Ob. 1 2
mf
Cl. (B♭) 1 2
Bn. 1 2
Hn. 1 2
Hn. 3 4
Timp.
Tamb.
pp
Tgl. Cymb.
131
Vn. 1
ppp
Vn. 2
ppp
Va.
arco
Vc.
pp
Cb.

139
Picc.
Fl. 1 2
mf
Ob. 1 2
mf
Cl. (B♭) 1 2
Bn. 1 2
p
1.
p
Hn. 1 2 3 4
Timp.
Tamb.
Tgl. Cymb.
139
Vn. 1 2
p
p
arco
Va.
p
Vc.
p
Cb.

146
Picc.
mf cresc. poco a poco
Fl. 1 2
a2
mf cresc. poco a poco
Ob. 1 2
a2
mf marc. assai
Cl. (B♭) 1 2
a2
mf marc. assai
Bn. 1 2
Hn. 1 2
3 4
Timp.
p
Tamb.
pp
p
Tgl. Cymb.
146
Vn. 1
2
Va.
Vc.
Cb.

154
Picc.
Fl. 1 2
Ob. 1 2
Cl. (B♭) 1 2
Bn. 1 2
Hn. 1 2
Hn. 3 4
Timp.
Tamb.
Tgl. Cymb.
Vn. 1
Vn. 2
Va.
Vc.
Cb.
cresc. poco a poco
f

167
162
Picc.
Fl. 1 2
Ob. 1 2
ff marcatissimo
Cl. (B♭) 1 2
ff marcatissimo
Bn. 1 2
Hn. 1 2 3 4
a2
3.
Timp.
Tamb.
Tgl. Cymb.
167
162
Vn. 1 2
Va.
Vc.
Cb.
arco

172
Picc.
Fl. 1 2
Ob. 1 2
Cl. (B♭) 1 2
Bn. 1 2
Hn. 1 2
Hn. 3 4
Timp.
Tamb.
Tgl. Cymb.
Vn. 1
Vn. 2
Va.
Vc.
Cb.
a2
pizz. div.
pizz.

181
Picc.
Fl. 1 2
Ob. 1 2
Cl. (B♭) 1 2
p dolce
1.
Bn. 1 2
p
1.
Hn. 1 2
p
3 4
Timp.
p
Tamb.
Tgl. Cymb.
p
181
unis.
p
arco
Vn. 1
unis.
p
arco
2
arco spiccato assai
Va.
ff dim.
pizz.
arco
Vc.
p
pizz.
Cb.
p

189
Picc.
Fl. 1 2
Ob. 1 2
Cl. (B♭) 1 2
Bn. 1 2
Hn. 1 2
Hn. 3 4
Timp.
Tamb.
Tgl. Cymb.
Vn. 1
Vn. 2
Va.
Vc.
Cb.
mf
f
p
pizz.
arco

195
Picc.
Fl. 1 2
Ob. 1 2
Cl. (B♭) 1 2
Bn. 1 2
Hn. 1 2
3 4
Timp.
Tamb.
Tgl. Cymb.
Vn. 1
2
Va.
Vc.
Cb.
mf
cresc. molto
a2
f marc.
cresc.
p
p cresc.
pizz.
arco

201
Picc.
Fl. 1 2
Ob. 1 2
2. to E. H.
Cl. (B♭) 1 2
to A cl.
Bn. 1 2
a2
Hn. 1 2
Hn. 3 4
Timp.
Tamb.
Tgl. Cymb.
201
Vn. 1
Vn. 2
Va.
Vc.
Cb.
pizz.
arco

2.

Andantino

7
Picc.
Fl. 1 2
Ob.
E. H.
p dolce
Cl. (A) 1 2
1.
pp
Bn. 1 2
Hn. 1 2 3 4
Tpt. 1 2
Trb. 1 2 Bass Tuba
Timp.
Tgl.
Hp.
Vn. 1
3 soli
Vn. 2
2 soli
Va.
Vc.
div.
3 soli arco
Cb.

15
Ob.
p con espress. e dolce
E. H.
mf
Cl. (A) 1 2
p
Bn. 1 2
p
Hp.
p
15
Vn. 1
Vn. 2
Va.
pizz. tutti
Vc.
p
Cb.
21
p cantabile espress.
21
sul a
pp
pp

27
31
Picc.
Fl. 1 2
a2
mf
Ob.
mf
E. H.
mf
Cl. (A) 1 2
mf
Bn. 1 2
mf
Hn. 1 2 3 4
Tpt. 1 2
Trb. 1 2
Bass Tuba
Timp.
Tgl.
pp
Hp.
f
27
31
Vn. 1 2
ord.
f
pizz.
f
Va.
pizz.
f
Vc.
div.
arco
f cantabile e rubato
(pizz.)
f
Cb.
pizz.
f

32
Picc.
Fl. 1 2
Ob.
E. H.
Cl. (A) 1 2
Bn. 1 2
Hn. 1 2 3 4
1.
p
3.
p
Tpt. 1 2
Trb. 1 2
Bass Tuba
Timp.
Tgl.
Hp.
32
Vn. 1 2
Va.
Vc.
Cb.

37
Picc.
Fl. 1 2
Ob.
p dolce
E. H.
Cl. (A) 1 2
dim.
p
Bn. 1 2
dim.
p
Hn. 1 2
dim.
p
3 4
p
Tpt. 1 2
Trb. 1 2
Bass Tuba
Timp.
Tgl.
Hp.
dim.
p
37
sul g
Vn. 1
2
dim.
p
Va.
Vc.
dim.
p
Cb.
dim.
p

42
Allegro vivo ♩ = 152
Picc.
Fl. 1 2
Ob.
E. H.
p dolce
Cl. (A) 1 2
to B♭ cl.
Bn. 1 2
a2
p
Hn. 1 2 3 4
Tpt. 1 2
Trb. 1 2
Bass Tuba
Timp.
Tgl.
ppp
to tamb.
Hp.
42
Allegro vivo ♩ = 152
ord.
Vn. 1 2
pp
p sempre
arco
Va.
p sempre
Vc.
pp
Cb.

48
1.
Cl. (B♭) 1 2
mf
Bn. 1 2
Timp.
48
Vn. 1 2
Va.
Vc.
Cb.
52
Picc.
mf
Fl. 1 2
Ob.
E. H.
f marc.
Cl. (B♭) 1 2
a2
f marc.
Bn. 1 2
f marc.
3
Timp.
52
Vn. 1 2
Va.
mf
unis. arco
Vc.
mf
arco
Cb.
p

57
Picc.
1.
Fl. 1 2
mf
a2
Ob.
E. H.
Cl. (B♭) 1 2
Bn. 1 2
Hn. 1 2
3 4
Tpt. 1 2
Trb. 1 2
Bass Tuba
Timp.
Tamb.
Hp.
57
Vn. 1
2
Va.
Vc.
Cb.

64
61
Picc.
Fl. 1 2
Ob.
E. H.
Cl. (B♭) 1 2
Bn. 1 2
Hn. 1 2
Hn. 3 4
Tpt. 1 2
Trb. 1 2
Bass Tuba
Tuba
Timp.
Tamb.
Hp.
f marc.
f marc.
f marc.
f marc.
f marc.
f
f
f
pp
mf
p
64
61
Vn. 1
Vn. 2
arco
Va.
Vc.
Cb.
f
f
f
f
f

65
Picc.
Fl. 1 2
Ob.
E. H.
Cl. (B♭) 1 2
Bn. 1 2
Hn. 1 2
3 4
Tpt. 1 2
Trb. 1 2
Bass Tuba
Timp.
Tamb.
Hp.
65
Vn. 1
2
Va.
Vc.
Cb.

69
Picc.
Fl. 1 2
Ob.
E. H.
Cl. (B♭) 1 2
Bn. 1 2
Hn. 1 2
3 4
Tpt. 1 2
Trb. 1 2
Bass Tuba
Timp.
Tamb.
Hp.
69
Vn. 1
2
Va.
Vc.
Cb.
ff
f
f marc.
a2
3
non div.
ff sempre

73
Picc.
Fl. 1 2
Ob.
E. H.
Cl. (B♭) 1 2
Bn. 1 2
Hn. 1 2
Hn. 3 4
Tpt. 1 2
Trb. 1 2
Bass Tuba
Timp.
Tamb.
Hp.
73
Vn. 1
Vn. 2
Va.
Vc.
Cb.

80
77
Picc.
Fl. 1 2
mf
Ob.
mf
E. H.
mf
Cl. (B♭) 1 2
mf
Bn. 1 2
Hn. 1 2
mf
3 4
mf
Tpt. 1 2
Trb. 1 2
Bass
Tuba
Timp.
Tamb.
Hp.
80
77
Vn. 1
mf
2
mf
Va.
mf
dim.
Vc.
mf
dim.
Cb.
mf
dim.

82
Picc.
Fl. 1 2
Ob.
E. H.
Cl. (B♭) 1 2
Bn. 1 2
Hn. 1 2
3 4
3.
Tpt. 1 2
Trb. 1 2
Bass Tuba
Timp.
Tamb.
Hp.
82
Vn. 1
2
Va.
Vc.
Cb.
p
dim.

87
accel.
Picc.
Fl. 1 2
Ob.
E. H.
Cl. (B♭) 1 2
Bn. 1 2
Hn. 1 2 3 4
Tpt. 1 2
Trb. 1 2
Bass Tuba
Timp.
Tamb.
Hp.
Vn. 1 2
Va.
Vc.
Cb.
pp cresc. poco a poco
p cresc. poco a poco
ppp cresc. poco a poco
mp cresc.
mf
sf
to ob.
to A cl.

3.

Allegro 𝅗𝅥. = 69
Piccolo
Flute 1 2
Oboe 1 2
Clarinet (A) 1 2
Bassoon 1 2
Horn (F) 1 2 3 4
Trumpet (C) 1 2
Trombone 1 2
Bass Tuba
Timpani
Triangle Cymbals
Snare Drum Bass Drum
Harp
Allegro 𝅗𝅥. = 69
Violin 1 2
Viola
Violoncello
Contrabass
a2
flt.
pp
p
mf
f
ff

11
Picc.
Fl. 1 2
Ob. 1 2
Cl. (A) 1 2
Bn. 1 2
Hn. 1 2
3 4
Tpt. 1 2
flt.
Trb. 1 2
Bass Tuba
Timp.
Tgl. Cymb.
S. D. B. D.
Hp.
Vn. 1
2
Va.
Vc.
Cb.
tr
ff
f

20
Picc.
Fl. 1 2
Ob. 1 2
Cl. (A) 1 2
Bn. 1 2
Hn. 1 2
3 4
Tpt. 1 2
Trb. 1 2
Bass Tuba
Timp.
Tgl. Cymb.
S. D. B. D.
Hp.
20
Vn. 1
2
Va.
Vc.
Cb.

29
Picc.
Fl. 1 2
Ob. 1 2
Cl. (A) 1 2
Bn. 1 2
Hn. 1 2
3 4
Tpt. 1 2
flt.
Trb. 1 2
(a2)
Bass Tuba
Timp.
Tgl. Cymb.
S. D. B. D.
Hp.
29
Vn. 1
2
Va.
Vc.
Cb.
ff
f
tr

45
40
Picc.
Fl. 1 2
Ob. 1 2
Cl. (A) 1 2
Bn. 1 2
Hn. 1 2 3 4
Tpt. 1 2
Trb. 1 2
Bass Tuba
Timp.
Tgl. Cymb.
S. D. B. D.
Hp.
Vn. 1 2
Va.
Vc.
Cb.
tr
p
cresc.
2.
flt.
ppp
s. c. with stick
f
to glock.
div.

50
Picc.
Fl. 1 2
Ob. 1 2
cresc.
p
Cl. (A) 1 2
Bn. 1 2
1.
Hn. 1 2 3 4
Tpt. 1 2
Trb. 1 2
Bass Tuba
Timp.
Tgl. Cymb.
Glock.
Hp.
Vn. 1 2
Va.
Vc.
Cb.

61
Picc.
Fl. 1 2
Ob. 1 2
Cl. (A) 1 2
Bn. 1 2
Hn. 1 2 3 4
Tpt. 1 2
Trb. 1 2
Bass Tuba
Timp.
Tgl. Cymb.
Glock.
Hp.
Vn. 1 2
Va.
Vc.
Cb.
cresc.

69
Picc.
Fl. 1 2
Ob. 1 2
Cl. (A) 1 2
Bn. 1 2
Hn. 1 2
3 4
Tpt. 1 2
Trb. 1 2
Bass Tuba
Timp.
Tgl. Cymb.
Glock.
Hp.
Vn. 1
2
Va.
Vc.
Cb.
tr
p
cresc.
a2
1.
non div.
(non div.)
unis.
to S.D. & B. D.

81
80
Picc.
Fl. 1 2
Ob. 1 2
Cl. (A) 1 2
Bn. 1 2
Hn. 1 2
3 4
Tpt. 1 2
Trb. 1 2
Bass Tuba
Timp.
Tgl. Cymb.
S. D. B. D.
Hp.
Vn. 1
2
Va.
Vc.
Cb.
a2
ff
f
flt.
unis.
tr

90
Picc.
Fl. 1 2
Ob. 1 2
Cl. (A) 1 2
Bn. 1 2
Hn. 1 2 3 4
Tpt. 1 2
flt.
Trb. 1 2
Bass Tuba
Timp.
Tgl. Cymb.
S. D. B. D.
Hp.
90
Vn. 1 2
Va.
Vc.
Cb.

100
Picc.
Fl. 1 2
Ob. 1 2
Cl. (A) 1 2
Bn. 1 2
Hn. 1 2
Hn. 3 4
Tpt. 1 2
Trb. 1 2
Bass Tuba
Timp.
Tgl. Cymb.
S. D. B. D.
Hp.
Vn. 1
Vn. 2
Va.
Vc.
Cb.
a2
ff
f

109
Picc.
Fl. 1 2
Ob. 1 2
Cl. (A) 1 2
Bn. 1 2
Hn. 1 2 3 4
Tpt. 1 2
flt.
a2
Trb. 1 2
Bass Tuba
ff
Timp.
Tgl. Cymb.
S. D. B. D.
f
Hp.
109
Vn. 1 2
Va.
Vc.
Cb.
tr

121
117
Picc.
Fl. 1 2
Ob. 1 2
Cl. (A) 1 2
Bn. 1 2
Hn. 1 2 3 4
Tpt. 1 2
Trb. 1 2
Bass Tuba
Timp.
Tgl. Cymb.
S. D. B. D.
Hp.
Vn. 1 2
Va.
Vc.
Cb.
tr
flt.
a2
1.
p
f
pizz.

125
129
Cl. (A) 1 2
Bn. 1 2
Hn. 1 2
Hp.
2.
p
pp
Vn. 1 2
Va.
Vc.
Cb.
sul g
div.
unis.
134
to B♭ cl.
Hn. 3 4

4.

Presto 𝅗𝅥. = 100
Piccolo
Flute 1 2
Oboe 1 2
Clarinet (B♭) 1 2
Bassoon 1 2
a2
f
Horn (F) 1 2 3 4
Trumpet (C) 1 2
Trombone 1 2
Bass Tuba
Timpani
Snare Drum
pp
Triangle Tambourine
Cymbals Bass Drum
Harp
Presto 𝅗𝅥. = 100
Violin 1 2
saltando
p leggerissimo
Viola
pizz.
p
Violoncello
pizz.
ff
Contrabass

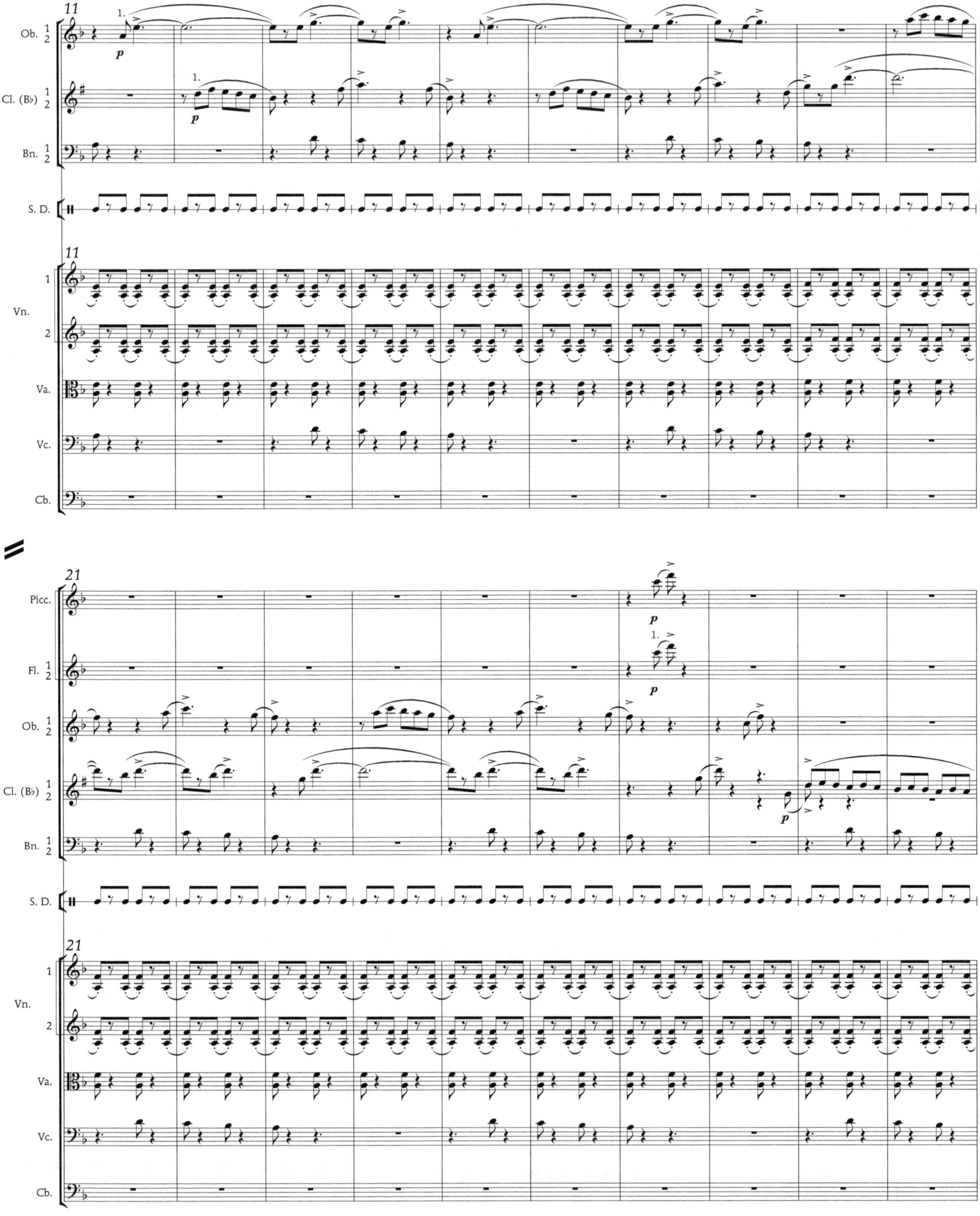
11
Ob. 1 2
Cl. (B♭) 1 2
Bn. 1 2
S. D.
Vn. 1 2
Va.
Vc.
Cb.
21
Picc.
Fl. 1 2

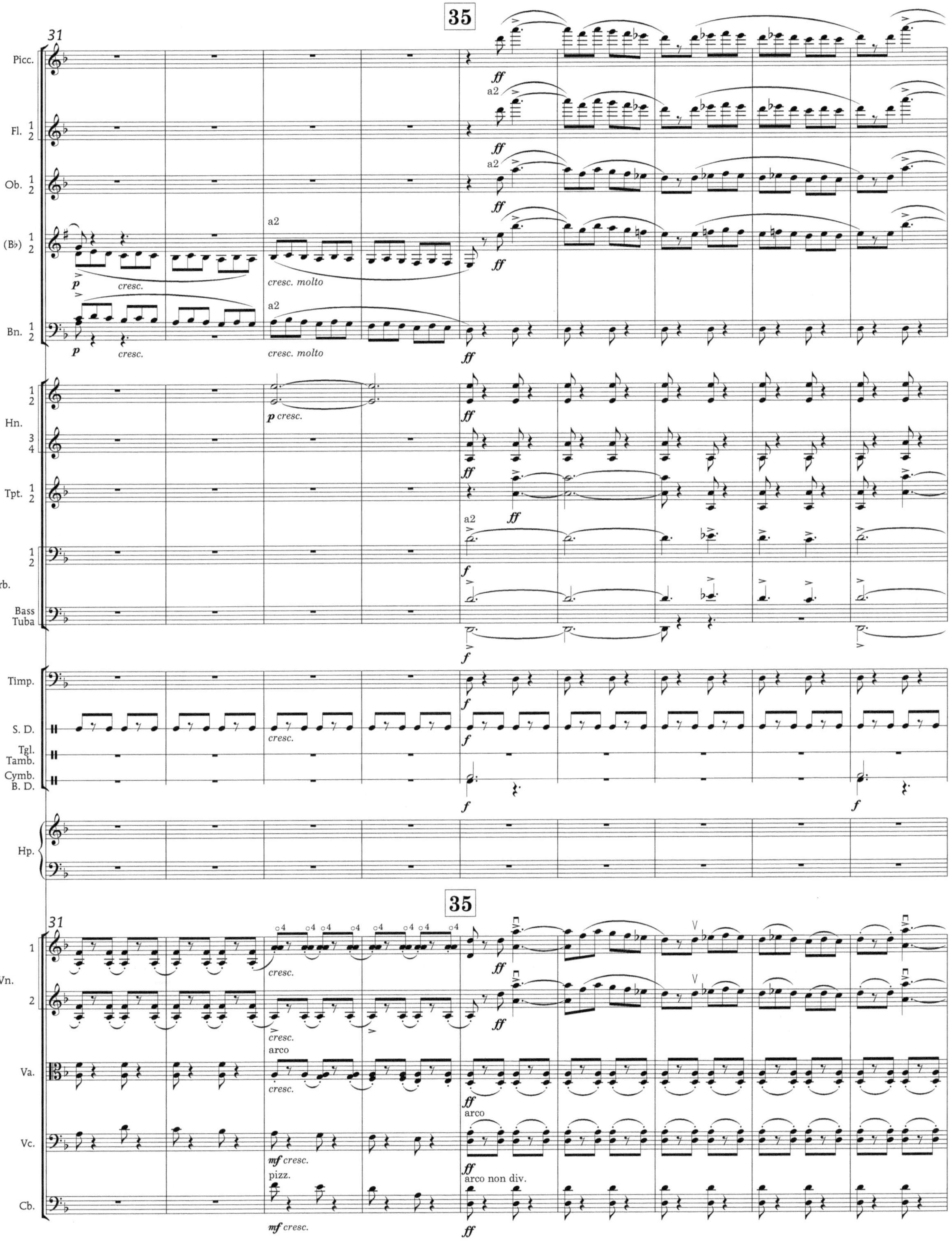
35
31
Picc.
Fl. 1 2
Ob. 1 2
Cl. (B♭) 1 2
Bn. 1 2
Hn. 1 2 3 4
Tpt. 1 2
Trb. 1 2
Bass Tuba
Timp.
S. D.
Tgl. Tamb.
Cymb. B. D.
Hp.
Vn. 1 2
Va.
Vc.
Cb.
a2
p
cresc.
cresc. molto
p cresc.
ff
f
mf cresc.
pizz.
arco
arco non div.

40
Picc.
Fl. 1 2
Ob. 1 2
Cl. (B♭) 1 2
Bn. 1 2
Hn. 1 2
Hn. 3 4
Tpt. 1 2
Trb. 1 2
Bass Tuba
Timp.
S. D.
Tgl. Tamb.
Cymb. B. D.
f
f
Hp.
40
Vn. 1
Vn. 2
Va.
Vc.
Cb.

55
49
Picc.
Fl. 1 2
Ob. 1 2
Cl. (B♭) 1 2
Bn. 1 2
Hn. 1 2 3 4
Tpt. 1 2
Trb. 1 2
B. T.
Bass Tuba
Timp.
S. D.
Tgl. Tamb.
Cymb. B. D.
Hp.
55
49
Vn. 1 2
Va.
Vc.
Cb.

58
Picc.
Fl. 1 2
Ob. 1 2
Cl. (B♭) 1 2
Bn. 1 2
f marc assai
Hn. 1 2 3 4
2.
4.
Tpt. 1 2
Trb. 1 2
Bass Tuba
Timp.
S. D.
Tgl. Tamb.
Cymb. B. D.
Hp.
Vn. 1 2
Va.
Vc.
Cb.
pizz.
arco
saltando
sf
f
mf
sfp
ff

68
Picc.
Fl. 1 2
Ob. 1 2
Cl. (B♭) 1 2
Bn. 1 2
Hn. 1 2
3 4
Tpt. 1 2
Trb. 1 2
Bass Tuba
Timp.
S. D.
Tgl. Tamb.
Cymb. B. D.
Hp.
Vn. 1
2
Va.
Vc.
Cb.
div.

77
Picc.
Fl. 1 2
Ob. 1 2
Cl. (B♭) 1 2
a2
to A cl.
Bn. 1 2
Hn. 1 2 3 4
Tpt. 1 2
Trb. 1 2
Bass Tuba
Timp.
S. D.
Tgl. Tamb.
Cymb. B. D.
Hp.
77
Vn. 1 2
Va.
Vc.
Cb.

86
89
Picc.
Fl. 1 2
Ob. 1 2
Cl. (A) 1 2
Bn. 1 2
p
Hn. 1 2
3 4
coperti
Timp.
p
Vn. 1
2
con sord.
Va.
arco
f
Vc.
pizz.
mf
Cb.
95
unis.
p

105
113
Picc.
Fl. 1 2
Ob. 1 2
a2
Cl. (A) 1 2
Bn. 1 2
a2
Hn.
1 2
3 4
a2
Tpt. 1 2
Trb.
1 2
1.
Bass Tuba
Timp.
S. D.
Tgl. Tamb.
Cymb. B. D.
Hp.
105
113
Vn.
1
2
senza sord.
Va.
Vc.
arco saltando
Cb.

115
Picc.
a2
Fl. 1 2
Ob. 1 2
Cl. (A) 1 2
Bn. 1 2
Hn. 1 2
3 4
Tpt. 1 2
Trb. 1 2
Bass Tuba
Timp.
S. D.
Tgl. Tamb.
Cymb. B. D.
Hp.
115
Vn. 1
2
Va.
Vc.
Cb.
f
sf

124
Picc.
Fl. 1 2
Ob. 1 2
Cl. (A) 1 2
Bn. 1 2
Hn. 1 2 3 4
Tpt. 1 2
Trb. 1 2
Bass Tuba
Timp.
S. D.
Tgl. Tamb.
Cymb. B. D.
Hp.
124
Vn. 1 2
Va.
Vc.
Cb.
f
sf
dim.

137
Moderato alla breve 𝅗𝅥 = 100 (𝅗𝅥 = 𝅗𝅥.)
133
Picc.
Fl. 1 2
Ob. 1 2
1.
p dolce
2. to E. H.
Cl. (A) 1 2
p
Bn. 1 2
p
Hn. 1 2
1.
p
3 4
Tpt. 1 2
Trb. 1 2
Bass Tuba
senza coperti
Timp.
S. D.
Tgl. Tamb.
to glock.
Cymb. B. D.
Hp.
p
137
Moderato alla breve 𝅗𝅥 = 100 (𝅗𝅥 = 𝅗𝅥.)
133
Vn. 1
pizz.
p
2
pizz.
p
Va.
p dolce e cantabile
Vc.
p dolce
Cb.
pizz.
p

141
Ob.
Cl. (A) 1 2
Bn. 1 2
Hn. 1 2
Hp.
Vn. 1 2
Va.
Vc.
Cb.
150
E. H.
p dolce e cantabile
arco
tr
pizz.
cantabile

160
Picc.
Fl. 1 2
Ob.
E. H.
dim.
Cl. (A) 1 2
dim.
Bn. 1 2
dim.
Hn. 1 2 3 4
Tpt. 1 2
Trb. 1 2
Bass Tuba
Timp.
S. D.
Tgl. Tamb.
Glock.
Hp.
160
Vn. 1 2
Va.
div.
Vc.
dim.
Cb.

169

173
Picc.
Fl. 1 2
Ob.
E. H.
Cl. (A) 1 2
Bn. 1 2
Hn. 1 2
3 4
Tpt. 1 2
Trb. 1 2
Bass Tuba
Timp.
S. D.
Tgl. Tamb.
Glock.
Hp.
8va
173
Vn. 1
2
tr
Va.
Vc.
Cb.

177
Picc.
Fl. 1 2
Ob.
E. H.
Cl. (A) 1 2
Bn. 1 2
Hn. 1 2
3 4
Tpt. 1 2
Trb. 1 2
Bass Tuba
Timp.
S. D.
Tgl. Tamb.
Glock.
Hp.
177
Vn. 1
2
Va.
Vc.
Cb.

181
Picc.
Fl. 1 2
Ob.
E. H.
Cl. (A) 1 2
Bn. 1 2
Hn. 1 2
Hn. 3 4
Tpt. 1 2
Trb. 1 2
Bass Tuba
Timp.
S. D.
Tgl. Tamb.
Glock.
Hp.
181
Vn. 1
Vn. 2
Va.
Vc.
div.
saltando
p
pizz.
Cb.

185
Picc.
Fl. 1 2
Ob.
p dolce
E. H.
Cl. (A) 1 2
to B♭ cl.
Bn. 1 2
Hn. 1 2 3 4
p
1.
Tpt. 1 2
Trb. 1 2
Bass Tuba
Timp.
S. D.
dim.
pp
Tgl. Tamb.
to cymb. & b.d.
Glock.
Hp.
8va
dim.
p
185
Vn. 1 2
saltando
p
Va.
arco
p
Vc.
arco
p
Cb.
arco
p

190
Picc.
Fl. 1 2
Ob.
E. H.
p dolce
Cl. (B♭) 1 2
Bn. 1 2
1.
p
Hn. 1 2 3 4
Tpt. 1 2
Trb. 1 2
Bass Tuba
Timp.
S. D.
Tgl. Tamb.
Cymb. B. D.
Hp.
190
Vn. 1 2
Va.
Vc.
p
Cb.

196
Picc.
Fl. 1 2
Ob.
E. H.
to ob.
Cl. (B♭) 1 2
Bn. 1 2
Hn. 1 2 3 4
Tpt. 1 2
Trb. 1 2
Bass Tuba
Timp.
S. D.
Tgl. Tamb.
Cymb. B. D.
Hp.
tacet
196
Vn. 1 2
Va.
pizz.
Vc.
pp
Cb.
pp

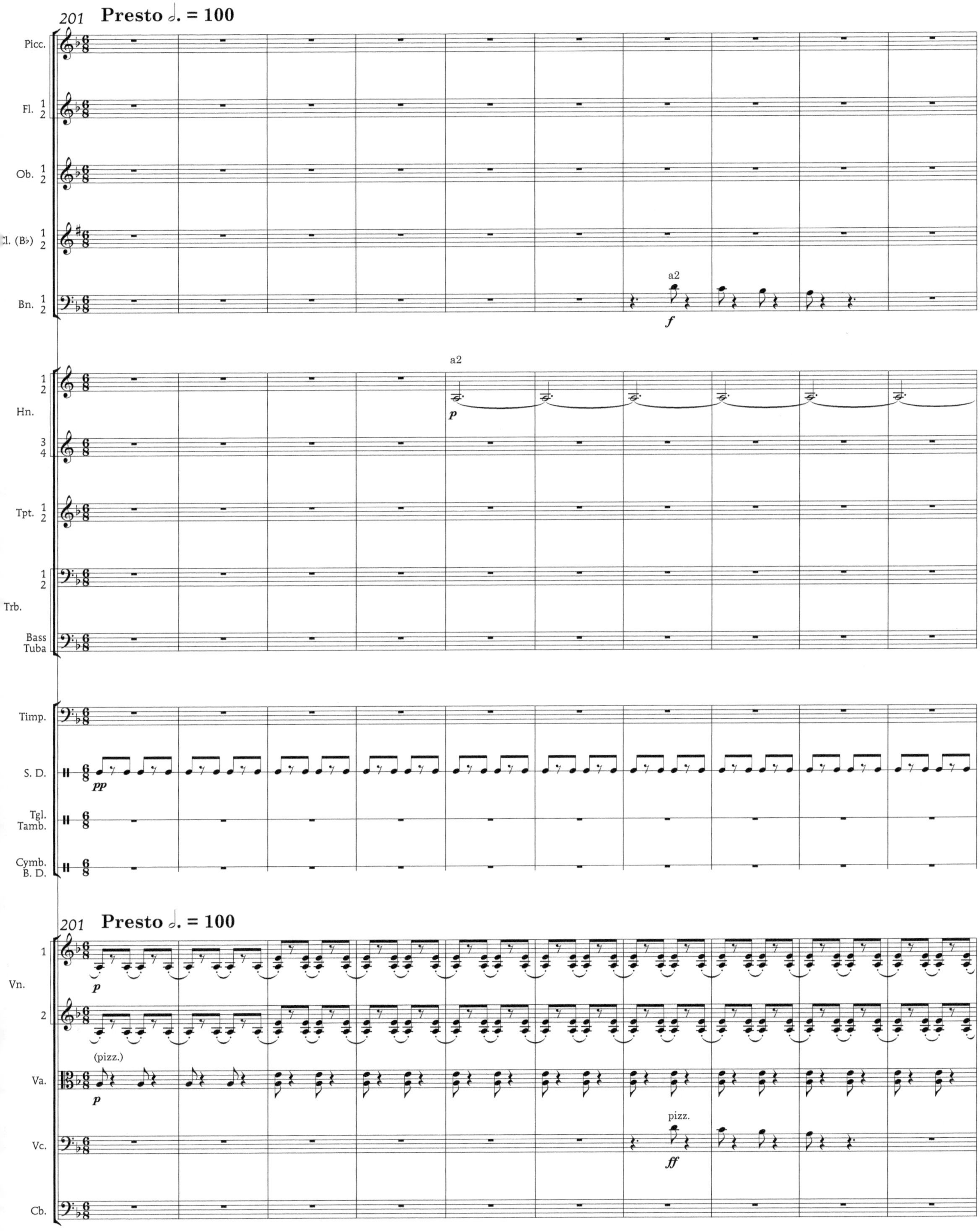

201 Presto 𝅗𝅥. = 100
Picc.
Fl. 1 2
Ob. 1 2
Cl. (B♭) 1 2
Bn. 1 2
a2
f
Hn. 1 2 3 4
a2
p
Tpt. 1 2
Trb. 1 2
Bass Tuba
Timp.
S. D.
pp
Tgl. Tamb.
Cymb. B. D.
201 Presto 𝅗𝅥. = 100
Vn. 1 2
p
(pizz.)
Va.
p
pizz.
Vc.
ff
Cb.

211
Picc.
Fl. 1 2
Ob. 1 2
Cl. (B♭) 1 2
Bn. 1 2
Hn. 1 2 3 4
a2
Tpt. 1 2
Trb. 1 2
Bass Tuba
Timp.
S. D.
Tgl. Tamb.
Cymb. B. D.
211
Vn. 1 2
Va.
Vc.
Cb.

221
Picc.
Fl. 1 2
Ob. 1 2
Cl. (B♭) 1 2
Bn. 1 2
Hn. 1 2
3 4
Tpt. 1 2
Trb. 1 2
Bass Tuba
Timp.
S. D.
Tgl. Tamb.
Cymb. B. D.
221
Vn. 1
2
Va.
Vc.
Cb.

237
231
Picc.
Fl. 1 2
Ob. 1 2
Cl. (B♭) 1 2
Bn. 1 2
Hn. 1 2
3 4
Tpt. 1 2
Trb. 1 2
Bass Tuba
Timp.
S. D.
Tgl. Tamb.
Cymb. B. D.
Vn. 1
2
Va.
Vc.
Cb.
a2
ff
p
f
mf
cresc.
cresc. molto
p cresc.
mf cresc.
arco
pizz.
arco non div.

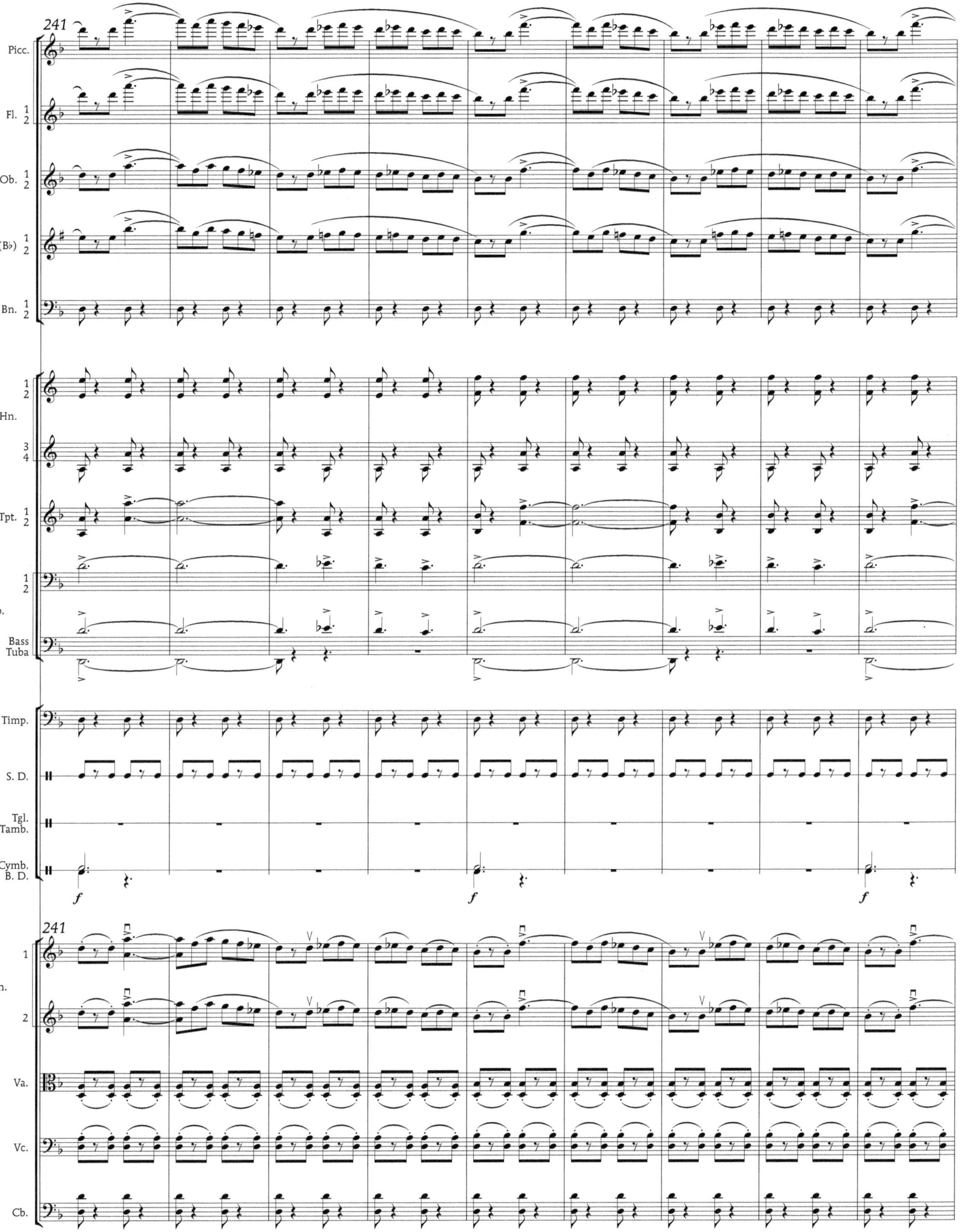
241
Picc.
Fl. 1 2
Ob. 1 2
Cl. (B♭) 1 2
Bn. 1 2
Hn. 1 2
3 4
Tpt. 1 2
Trb. 1 2
Bass Tuba
Timp.
S. D.
Tgl. Tamb.
Cymb. B. D.
f
f
f
241
Vn. 1
2
Va.
Vc.
Cb.

42226

42226

86

42226

278
Picc.
Fl. 1 2
Ob. 1 2
Cl. (B♭) 1 2
Bn. 1 2
Hn. 1 2
Hn. 3 4
Tpt. 1 2
Trb. 1 2
Bass Tuba
Timp.
S. D.
Tgl. Tamb.
Cymb. B. D.
a2
f
mf
ff
278
Vn. 1
Vn. 2
Va.
Vc.
Cb.

88

291

42226

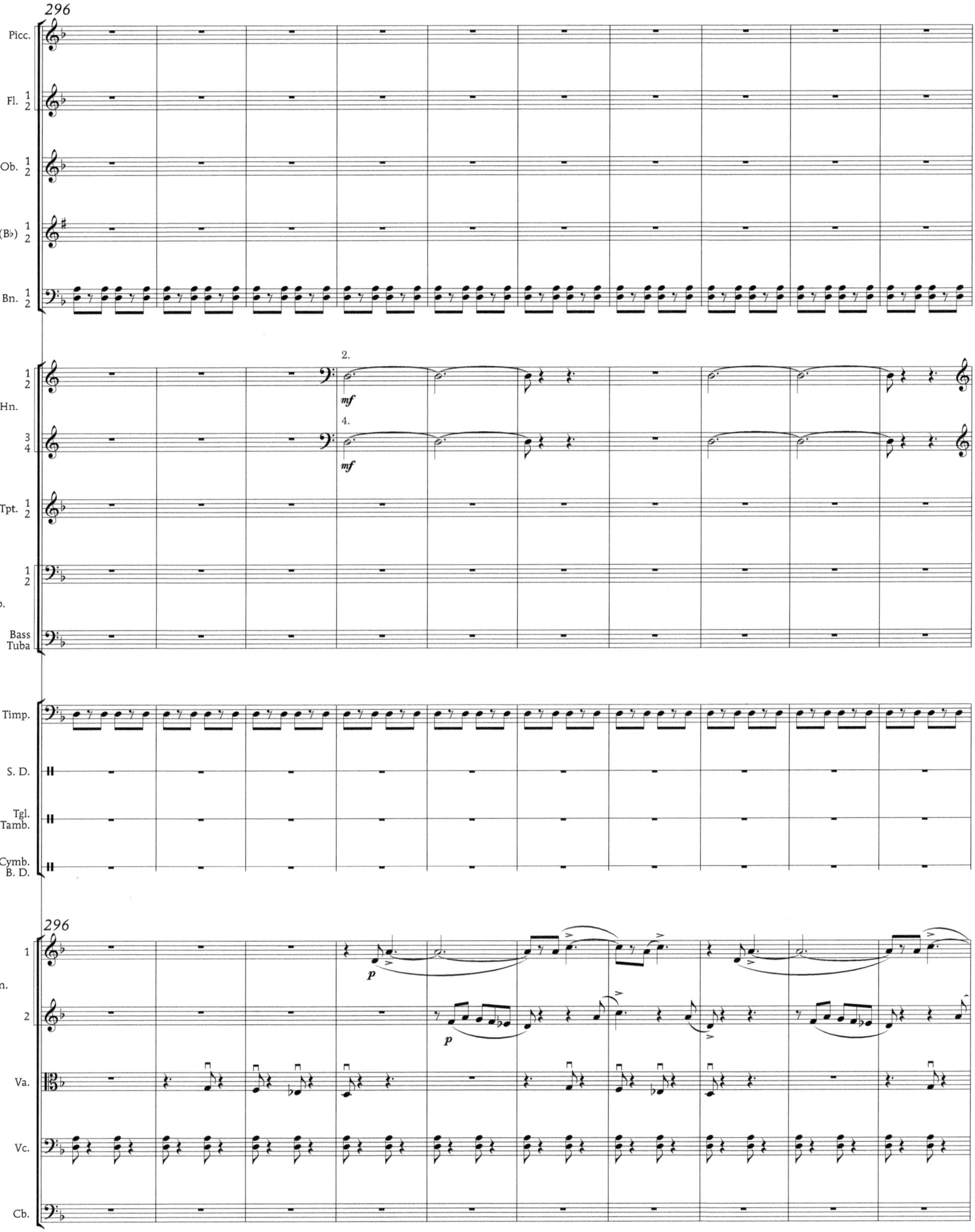
296
Picc.
Fl. 1 2
Ob. 1 2
Cl. (B♭) 1 2
Bn. 1 2
Hn. 1 2
2.
mf
Hn. 3 4
4.
mf
Tpt. 1 2
Trb. 1 2
Bass Tuba
Timp.
S. D.
Tgl. Tamb.
Cymb. B. D.
296
Vn. 1
p
Vn. 2
p
Va.
Vc.
Cb.

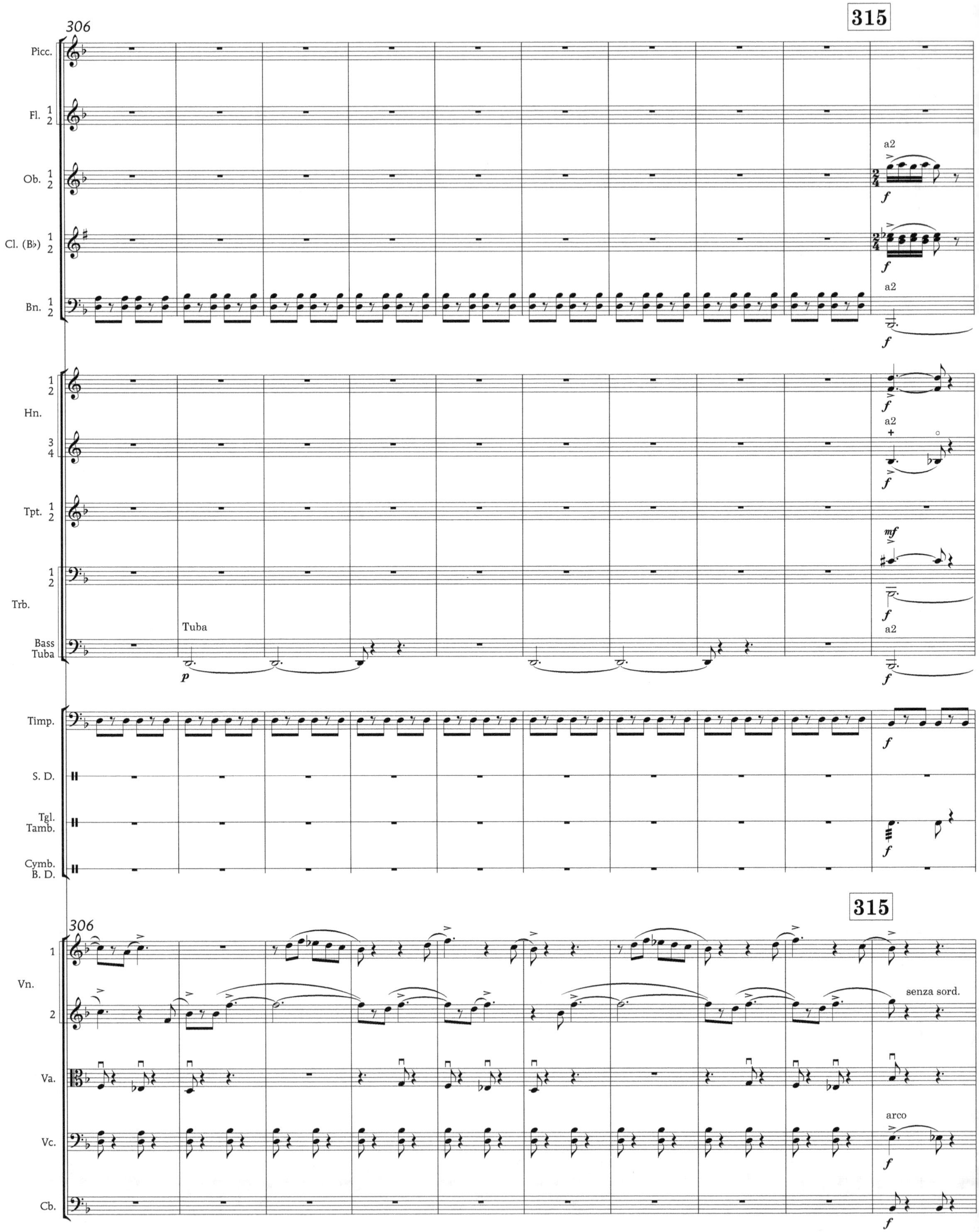
306
315
Picc.
Fl. 1 2
Ob. 1 2
a2
f
Cl. (B♭) 1 2
Bn. 1 2
Hn. 1 2
Hn. 3 4
Tpt. 1 2
mf
Trb. 1 2
Bass Tuba
Tuba
p
Timp.
S. D.
Tgl. Tamb.
Cymb. B. D.
Vn. 1
Vn. 2
senza sord.
Va.
Vc.
arco
Cb.

316
Picc.
ff
a2
Fl. 1 2
Ob. 1 2
Cl. (B♭) 1 2
Bn. 1 2
Hn. 1 2 3 4
Tpt. 1 2
sf
Trb. 1 2
Bass Tuba
Timp.
S. D.
Tgl. Tamb.
Cymb. B. D.
316
Vn. 1 2
Va.
f
Vc.
Cb.

325
Picc.
ff
Fl. 1 2
Ob. 1 2
Cl. (B♭) 1 2
to A cl.
Bn. 1 2
Hn. 1 2
3 4
3.
Tpt. 1 2
sf
Trb. 1 2
Bass Tuba
senza coperti
Timp.
S. D.
Tgl. Tamb.
Cymb. B. D.
325
Vn. 1 2
f
Va.
Vc.
Cb.

339 Allegro con spirito ♩ = 152
334
Picc.
Fl. 1 2
Ob. 1 2
Cl. (A) 1 2
Bn. 1 2
Hn. 1 2
3 4
Tpt. 1 2
Trb. 1 2
Bass Tuba
Timp.
S. D.
Tgl. Tamb.
Cymb. B. D.
339 Allegro con spirito ♩ = 152
334
pizz.
Vn. 1
2
Va.
Vc.
Cb.

340
Picc.
Fl. 1 2
Ob. 1 2
a2
Cl. (A) 1 2
Bn. 1 2
Hn. 1 2
3 4
Tpt. 1 2
Trb. 1 2
Bass Tuba
Timp.
S. D.
Tgl. Tamb.
Cymb. B. D.
340
Vn. 1
2
Va.
Vc.
Cb.

344
Picc.
Fl. 1 2
Ob. 1 2
Cl. (A) 1 2
Bn. 1 2
a2
Hn. 1 2
3 4
Tpt. 1 2
Trb. 1 2
Bass Tuba
marc. assai
Timp.
S. D.
Tgl. Tamb.
Cymb. B. D.
344
arco
Vn. 1 2
Va.
Vc.
Cb.

348
Picc.
Fl. 1 2
Ob. 1 2
Cl. (A) 1 2
Bn. 1 2
Hn. 1 2
3 4
Tpt. 1 2
Trb. 1 2
Bass Tuba
Timp.
S. D.
Tgl. Tamb.
Cymb. B. D.
348
Vn. 1
2
Va.
Vc.
Cb.

355 più animato ♩ = 176
352
Picc.
Fl. 1 2
Ob. 1 2
Cl. (A) 1 2
Bn. 1 2
a2
Hn. 1 2
3 4
Tpt. 1 2
Trb. 1 2
Bass Tuba
Timp.
S. D.
Tgl. Tamb.
Cymb. B. D.
355 più animato ♩ = 176
352
Vn. 1
2
Va.
Vc.
Cb.
pizz.

98

357

42226

364
363
Picc.
Fl. 1 2
Ob. 1 2
Cl. (A) 1 2
Bn. 1 2
Hn. 1 2
3 4
Tpt. 1 2
Trb. 1 2
Bass Tuba
Timp.
S. D.
Tgl. Tamb.
Cymb. B. D.
Vn. 1
2
Va.
Vc.
Cb.
a2
arco
f
mf
p

367
Picc.
Fl. 1 2
Ob. 1 2
Cl. (A) 1 2
Bn. 1 2
cresc.
Hn. 1 2
3 4
Tpt. 1 2
f
mf cresc.
Trb. 1 2
Bass Tuba
Timp.
S. D.
Tgl. Tamb.
Cymb. B. D.
p cresc.
367
Vn. 1
2
Va.
Vc.
Cb.

375
372
Picc.
Fl. 1 2
a2
Ob. 1 2
Cl. (A) 1 2
Bn. 1 2
ff
Hn. 1 2
Hn. 3 4
Tpt. 1 2
Trb. 1 2
Bass Tuba
mf cresc.
f
Timp.
S. D.
Tgl. Tamb.
Cymb. B. D.
Vn. 1
Vn. 2
Va.
Vc.
Cb.

379
376
Picc.
Fl. 1 2
a2
Ob. 1 2
Cl. (A) 1 2
Bn. 1 2
ff
Hn. 1 2 3 4
f
Tpt. 1 2
Trb. 1 2
Bass Tuba
Timp.
S. D.
Tgl. Tamb.
Cymb. B. D.
379
376
Vn. 1 2
Va.
Vc.
Cb.

380
Picc.
Fl. 1 2
a2
Ob. 1 2
Cl. (A) 1 2
Bn. 1 2
Hn. 1 2
Hn. 3 4
f
Tpt. 1 2
f
Trb. 1 2
Bass Tuba
Timp.
S. D.
Tgl. Tamb.
Cymb. B. D.
380
Vn. 1
Vn. 2
Va.
Vc.
Cb.

384
Picc.
Fl. 1 2
a2
Ob. 1 2
Cl. (A) 1 2
Bn. 1 2
a2
Hn. 1 2
Hn. 3 4
f
ff
Tpt. 1 2
Trb. 1 2
Bass Tuba
Timp.
S. D.
Tgl. Tamb.
Cymb. B. D.
384
Vn. 1
Vn. 2
div.
Va.
Vc.
Cb.

389
388
Picc.
Fl. 1 2
a2
Ob. 1 2
a2
Cl. (A) 1 2
a2
Bn. 1 2
sf
Hn. 1 2
sf
3 4
a2
sf
Tpt. 1 2
sf
Trb. 1 2
sf
Bass Tuba
sf
Timp.
sf
S. D.
Tgl. Tamb.
Cymb. B. D.
389
388
unis.
Vn. 1
div.
2
div.
unis.
Va.
Vc.
Cb.

392
Picc.
fff
Fl. 1 2
fff
a2
tr
Ob. 1 2
tr
Cl. (A) 1 2
tr
Bn. 1 2
Hn. 1 2
3 4
Tpt. 1 2
ff
Trb. 1 2
ff
a2
Bass Tuba
ff
Timp.
S. D.
ff
Tgl. Tamb.
ff
Cymb. B. D.
f
392
tr
Vn. 1
2
tr
Va.
tr
Vc.
Cb.

www.ingramcontent.com/pod-product-compliance
Lightning Source LLC
LaVergne TN
LVHW081319060426
835509LV00015B/1580